14.95

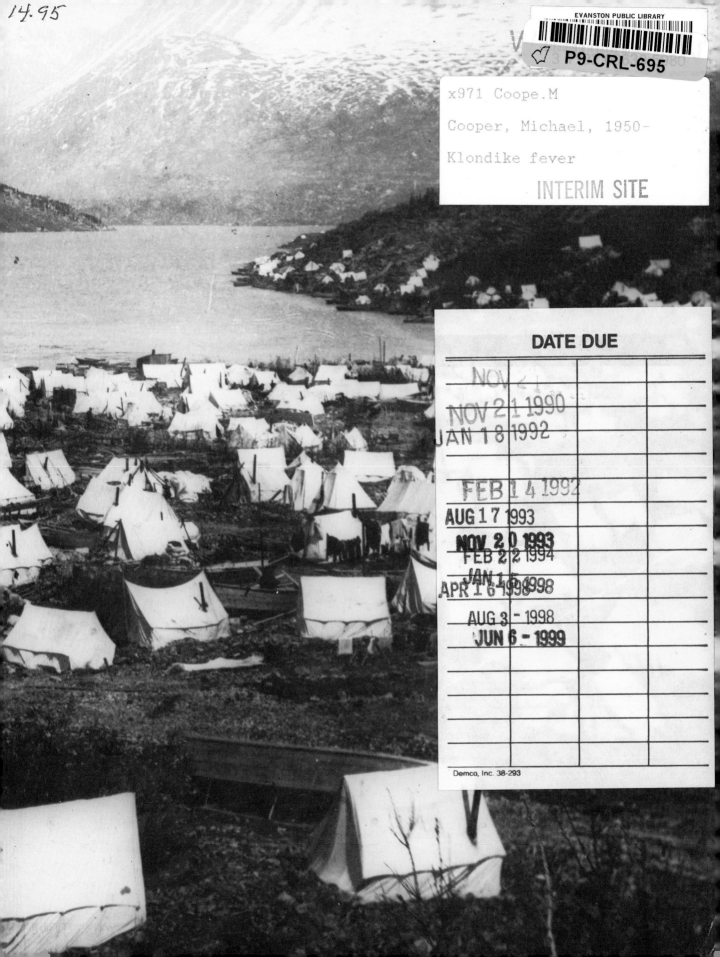

KLONDIKE FEVER

KLONDIKE FEVER

The Famous Gold Rush
of 1898

by Michael Cooper

Illustrated with photographs

Clarion Books

NEW YORK

Photo sources appear on page 73

Endleaf: Prospectors' camp on the shores of Lake Lindeman, 1898.
Photo courtesy of Royal Canadian Mounted Police.

Frontis: A rest stop on the trail to the Klondike.
Photo courtesy of the National Archives of Canada.

Clarion Books
a Houghton Mifflin Company imprint
52 Vanderbilt Avenue, New York, NY 10017
Text copyright © 1989 by Michael Cooper

Library of Congress Cataloging-in-Publication Data
Cooper, Michael, 1950–
Klondike Fever / by Michael Cooper.
p. cm.
Bibliography: p.
Includes index.
Summary: Traces the history of the Klondike gold rush of the late
1890s, describing the men responsible for the initial discovery, the
trail to the Klondike gold fields, and the explosive growth and
rapid demise of the gold rush town of Dawson.
ISBN 0-89919-803-1
1. Klondike River Valley (Yukon)—Gold discoveries—Juvenile
literature. [1. Klondike River Valley (Yukon)—Gold discoveries.]
I. Title.
F1095.K5C66 1989
971.9'1—dc 19   89-31117
                                         CIP
                                         AC

P 10 9 8 7 6 5 4 3 2 1

For Russell

Contents

The Yukon River, one of North America's longest rivers, was an important "highway" for gold seekers. These two men are pulling their boat ashore.

Discovering Gold

ONE MIDSUMMER day in 1896, on a creek so remote that it did not even have a name, Robert Henderson scooped up a pan of gravel and sand. As he peered into the pan, his eyes grew wide. Did he dare believe what he saw? There was one flake . . . now several flakes . . . of the precious metal that he had spent his life seeking. It was GOLD!

The discovery of these few flakes confirmed what the excited prospector had long suspected. Buried in this creek and in other creeks nearby were tens of millions of dollars worth of gold dust and gold nuggets. But as close as Henderson was to that fortune, he would not be the one who found it.

This lone prospector was an important, but unlucky, character in the story of the Klondike Gold Rush. Henderson grew up in Nova Scotia and began his gold-seeking career in the mountains of Colorado. After several luckless years there, the Canadian journeyed north almost to the Arctic Circle. Near the border between Alaska and Canada, Henderson began prospecting, or exploring, for gold in the many creeks that flow into the upper Yukon River.

For over two years, he had prospected in creek after creek and found nothing but disappointment.

But that midsummer day in 1896 his luck changed. After finding those first few flakes of gold in the creek, which he had hopefully named Gold Bottom, Henderson dug feverishly for several weeks. He unearthed over seven hundred and fifty dollars worth of gold flakes and gold nuggets. This was more money than most people in those days earned in a year. Henderson was feeling very lucky because his many years of hard work were finally paying off. But his luck did not last long.

Returning with supplies from the town of Fortymile, Henderson met George Washington Carmack and his two Indian companions, Jim and Charlie. Influenced by the growing number of white people in the region, Indians like Jim and Charlie had adopted white men's names. Henderson told the three men about his discovery. But Carmack, Jim, and Charlie were not prospectors, and they thought hunting gold was a waste of time. They were more interested in hunting moose.

For several days, the three companions stalked the large moose that fed on the willow trees growing along the creeks. But gold has a powerful allure, and the trio could not forget about Henderson's discovery. Curious to see if he had found more of the precious ore, they visited Henderson's camp.

During the visit, Jim and Charlie asked the prospector to sell them some tobacco. But Henderson, like many white people at the time, thought that Indians were inferior people and he treated them scornfully. No, he told them, he would not sell tobacco, or anything else, to Indians. That refusal might have cost Henderson the fortune he had sought for so many years. Charlie, Jim, and Carmack went away angry at Henderson.

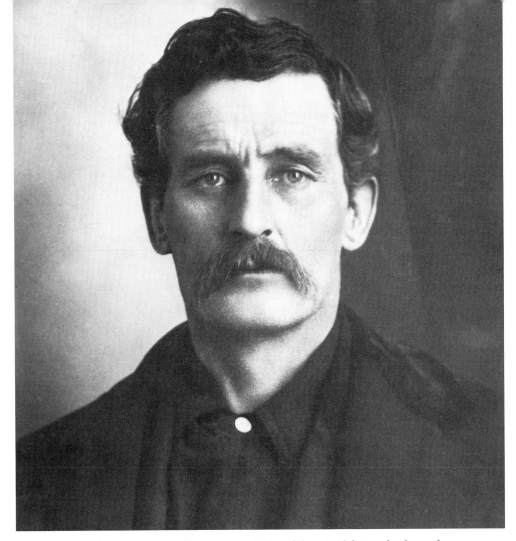

Robert Henderson helped start the Klondike Gold Rush, but the lifelong prospector found very little gold himself.

A few days later, the three men were camped on Rabbit Creek. While one of them was washing a pan in the clear water, he saw the glint of gold on the gravelly creek bottom. He reached into the shallow water and pulled out a thumb-sized nugget. With a whoop and a shout he called his two friends over. They scooped up a big handful of gravel; it contained nearly four dollars worth of gold. If one scoop yielded this much gold, they thought with growing excitement, the creek must be full of it. We're rich! the threesome realized, RICH!

Carmack hurried down river to Fortymile to file claims for himself, Jim, and Charlie. A claim is a legal right to mine gold, or other minerals, on a specific piece of land. After filing his claims, Carmack proudly walked into a smokey saloon full of miners. In a loud voice, he told the crowd that he had made one of the biggest gold strikes ever. His boast was greeted by a chorus of hoots and disbelief.

Why should anyone believe that this man had discovered gold? After all he was not a "sourdough," someone who has been a prospector for a long time. Carmack backed up his words by pulling out a small bag of gold nuggets. This was all the proof the prospectors needed. The next morning Fortymile was nearly deserted. Its citizens had rushed to stake claims on Rabbit Creek. The great Klondike Gold Rush had begun.

Before the Klondike Gold Rush, Fortymile was the largest town in northwestern Canada.

Carmack could have kept his gold strike a secret, at least for a while. But people who lived in that inhospitable land had a code that food, cabins, and even the exact location of a gold strike were freely shared. Despite that code, Carmack did not bother to travel the few miles to Gold Bottom Creek to tell Henderson of his discovery.

Some people believe Henderson was ignored because of his scornful treatment of Jim and Charlie. But there is no way of knowing exactly why Carmack neglected Henderson. What is known is that Henderson did not hear about the strike until the best claims had been taken. Many of the people whom Carmack did tell shared in the millions of dollars worth of gold that were dug from Rabbit Creek, which had been aptly renamed Bonanza Creek. *Bonanza* is a Spanish word that means the "source of wealth."

As news of the gold strike spread slowly throughout the region, more and more people joined the rush. The trading post owner in Fortymile loaded a steamboat full of food and mining equipment and steamed up the Yukon to the Klondike River. Near where the two rivers joined, he built a log trading post; this was the beginning of the famous gold-rush town of Dawson. Because Bonanza and other gold-laden creeks flow into the larger Klondike River, the whole region was called the Klondike.

From Dawson, rumors of the big gold strike drifted downstream two-hundred and twenty-five miles to Circle City, Alaska. The people there were used to hearing false rumors, so at first they didn't believe the stories about Bonanza Creek. But their curiosity soon got the better of them.

In cold and gloomy January the rush from Circle to Dawson began. Prospectors loaded food, tents, and mining equipment onto

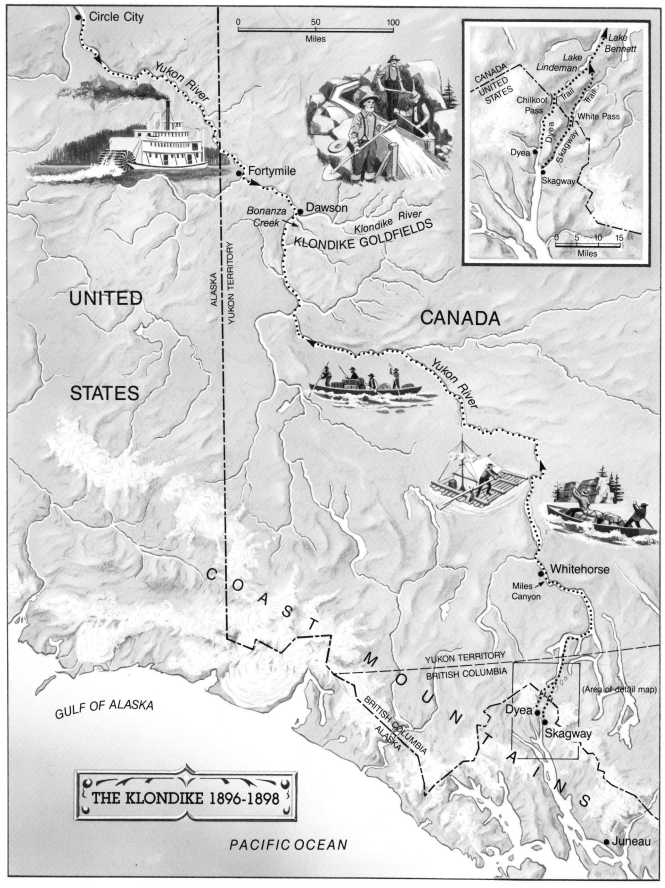

Circle City

Yukon River

50   100
Miles

Fortymile

Bonanza
Creek
Dawson

Klondike River
KLONDIKE GOLDFIELDS

ALASKA
YUKON TERRITORY

UNITED

STATES

CANADA

Yukon River

GULF OF ALASKA

C O A S T

M O U N T A I N S

Whitehorse

Miles
Canyon

YUKON TERRITORY
BRITISH COLUMBIA

BRITISH COLUMBIA
ALASKA

Dyea

(Area of detail map)

Skagway

THE KLONDIKE 1896-1898

PACIFIC OCEAN

Juneau

Map by George Buctel

Detail map:

Lake
Bennett

Lake
Lindeman

CANADA
UNITED
STATES

Trail

Chilkoot
Pass

Trail

Dyea

White Pass

Dyea

Skagway

Skagway

0   5   10   15
Miles

News of the gold strike reached Juneau, Alaska, by the winter of 1896–1897. These men are starting on the seven-hundred-mile trip to the Klondike.

sleds, which were pulled through the deep snow by dog teams. There was so much demand for sled dogs that the price for a dog jumped from fifty dollars to several hundred dollars. People who couldn't afford a team pulled their own sleds. By spring, Circle City was nearly a ghost town, while Dawson had become a sprawling tent city of fifteen hundred people.

The rush of gold seekers from Circle to Dawson was a trickle compared to the torrent that came later. Once people throughout Canada and the United States heard gold was being shoveled from Klondike creeks, the region was flooded by a wave of humanity.

In Seattle, crowds of curious people greeted the PORTLAND *and its cargo of Klondike gold.*

Klondike Fever Sweeps North America

"GOLD! GOLD! GOLD! GOLD! SIXTY-EIGHT RICH MEN ON THE STEAMER PORTLAND; STACKS OF YELLOW METAL!" This exuberant headline in a Seattle, Washington, newspaper hailed the arrival on July 17, 1897, of seven hundred thousand dollars worth of Klondike gold. Crowds of people mobbed the dock hoping to catch a glimpse of the precious cargo and the rich prospectors.

Just one day earlier, the steamship *Excelsior* caused a similar sensation when it arrived in San Francisco, California, with four hundred thousand dollars worth of Klondike gold.

News of the gold created a public frenzy that the newspapers dubbed "Klondike fever," and for months it was a front-page story. The *Seattle-Post-Intelligencer* interviewed anybody who knew anything about the remote section of Canada where the gold had been discovered. No one knew how much gold was there, but estimates were quite generous. One man said the Klondike was ten times richer than the big 1848 California gold strike.

Another said it was the best place in the world to make money. Everybody agreed it was a "new El Dorado," a legendary land of fabulous wealth and opportunity.

Such declarations in Seattle's and other newspapers spread Klondike fever far and wide. In the 1890s, newspapers were being read by more people than ever before. Articles about prospectors striking it rich proved to be such popular reading that editors dispatched teams of reporters, artists, and photographers to the northern goldfields. Their accounts of the new El Dorado were printed in newspapers around the world.

Enthusiastic newspaper headlines heralded the PORTLAND's *arrival.*

After hearing about the gold strike, hundreds of people in Victoria, British Columbia, rushed to buy mining permits.

In 1897, those newspaper articles read like fairy tales that had come true. For four years the United States had suffered one of its worst depressions ever. Tens of thousands of people were jobless or barely earning enough money to survive.

For people who were unemployed or earning only a few hundred dollars a year, the possibility of digging up thousands of dollars worth of gold was very appealing indeed. It was so appealing that everyone, it seemed, was going to the Klondike. In Seattle so many dock workers, laborers, and store clerks left low-paying jobs to seek their fortunes in the goldfields that the city had a serious labor shortage.

Articles about the gold rush appeared in publications all across the United States. This illustration of Chilkoot Pass in early 1897 appeared in an article in New York-based SCRIBNER'S *magazine.*

For many of these people, the hardships of the journey began even before they left home. Traveling to the Klondike was quite expensive, costing the average voyager fifteen hundred dollars or more. A steamship ticket cost one hundred and fifty dollars. Passengers also had to pay to ship their supplies. One steamship company charged ten cents a pound and limited each passenger to twelve hundred pounds of supplies.

Mining gold in the wilderness of northern Canada, where winters are long and frigid, required at least half a ton of supplies for each person. The prospectors who had been aboard the *Portland* gave the *Seattle Post-Intelligencer* a list of food and clothing that one person would need to live eighteen months in the Klondike. These supplies cost about one hundred and seventy-five dollars — and this did not include the shovels, picks, and pans needed to mine gold.

PROVISIONS
bacon, 200 pounds
flour, 800 pounds
assorted dry fruit, 150 pounds
corn meal, 200 pounds
rice, 50 pounds
coffee, parched, 75 pounds
tea, 40 pounds
sugar, 75 pounds
beans, 150 pounds
condensed milk, 1 case
assortment of evaporated vegetables and meats

CLOTHING
2 suits of corduroy
3 pairs rubber boots
3 pairs heavy shoes
3 dozen heavy woolen socks
1/2 dozen woolen mitts
3 pairs woolen gloves
3 suits heavy underwear

2 suits mackinaw
2 hats
4 heavy woolen shirts
1 heavy coat
3 pairs of heavy woolen blankets

Despite the expense, many people made the long and difficult journey to the Klondike. During the height of the gold rush, from mid-1897 through 1898, over one hundred thousand people set out for that unfamiliar land near the Arctic Circle. Some fifty thousand of those hardy men and women reached their destination.

These people who journeyed to the Klondike during the gold rush were called "Klondikers." Some were from Canada, but the majority of Klondikers were from the United States. The rush enticed people from all over the world, Norwegians, Scots, Greeks, Italians, and even a group of Maoris, an aboriginal people from New Zealand.

Backgrounds were as varied as nationalities. Some Klondikers were veterans of previous rushes in Colorado, Nevada, and South Dakota. Others were clerks, business people, teachers, and politicians. One of the more unusual Klondikers was an English nobleman, Lord Avenmore, who made the trip attended by several servants. Few of these people had experience mining gold or living out of doors.

Klondikers were mostly men, but passenger lists show that numerous women sailed on the first steamers to the goldfields. A list published in the *Seattle Post-Intelligencer* on July 23, 1897, named eighty-five passengers who sailed north on the steamer *Portland*. Fifteen of the passengers were women, and only three

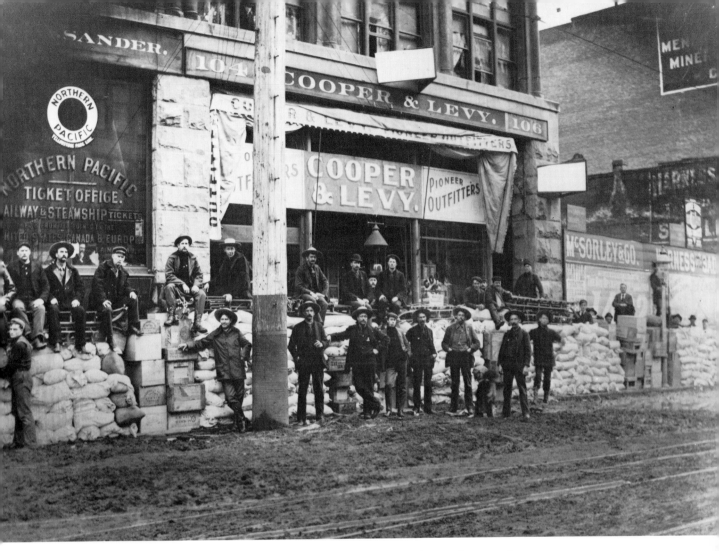

Seattle prospered as its merchants shipped tons of supplies to the Klondike.

were listed as traveling with their husbands. The newspaper article stated, "Many women are among the adventuring travelers. Some accompany husbands, others go to join loved ones amid the grinding hardships of life on the Yukon."

Seattle became the principal port for people and supplies bound for the Klondike. Within only six weeks after the *Portland* had arrived with its valuable cargo, nine thousand people and thirty-six thousand tons of food, lumber, tools, horses, dogs, and sundry supplies sailed north from Seattle's busy docks.

"SOO" LINE — Klondyke Bulletin

Kariboo Kootenay.

Vol. I, No. 10.   MINNEAPOLIS, MINN., FEB. 7, 1898.   New Subscribers Send 6cts. in Stamps.

ISSUED BY THE GENERAL PASSENGER DEPARTMENT. OF THE

Minneapolis, St. Paul & S. S. Marie Ry.

Send 6c. in Stamps to

W. R. CALLAWAY, G. P. A., Minneapolis, Minn.

INDEX.

GREENBACKS AT A PREMIUM.

A returned miner tells this story: "Greenbacks, contrary to the general rule, are at a premium over gold in the Klondyke country. We have to pay a $17 ounce for $15.25 in paper money, for, of course, everyone who thinks of coming out wants the paper money. I brought down all that I could get at a reasonable price, and also a few pounds of gold, which I have sold to the Bank of Montreal at $15.50. It was Bonanza gold, the finest standard of all, and I was rather disappointed in the price paid here."

EDMONTON

PROSPECTOR'S ROUTE

To the Great Gold Fields of the Northwest Territories—The Poor Man's Route to the New Klondykes—An Open Door.

A Visit to the Great Trade Centre and Outfitting Point in Alberta, Canada—The Explorations Which Demonstrate the Existence of Gold on Numerous Streams—Going to Edmonton by Rail and the Routes to Take From There—Gold Seekers Already There in Large Numbers Starting for the Winter Trip—Rich Strikes in Prospect—How to Outfit and Save Duties—The Gateway to the Coming Gold Mines.

(By permission St. Paul Pioneer Press, Jan. 31, '98.)

EDMONTON, ALBERTA, CANADA, January 27, 1898.

In the over one hundred years of its existence, important as it has been as a trade centre for the Canadian Northwest, the enterprising city of Edmonton has never enjoyed such prominence and trade as has been thrust upon her during the past twelve months.

Edmonton is located on the Saskatchewan River 191 miles north of the main line of the Canadian Pacific Railway upon the Calgary and Edmonton Branch, of which it is the terminus. It is 2,354 miles from Montreal, 930 miles from Winnipeg, and 1,340 from St. Paul and Minneapolis. It is reached from the Twin Cities via the SOO-PACIFIC, and its connection with the Canadian Pacific. You can go from the Twin Cities to Edmonton with but one change of cars.

ESTABLISHED THE LAST CENTURY.

Over one hundred years ago Edmonton was established as a trading post and notwithstanding it has had railroad communications with the outside world for but seven years, it has maintained a commercial importance beyond that of any town of its size in North America, and greater than many towns ten times its size. This is because it has been the gateway for the operations of hunters, trappers and Indian traders for one hundred years, and their natural market; because it is in the very heart of a most prolific agricultural and grazing district, and absolutely within the most extensive gold bearing region on the face of the globe, a combination which it is

This booklet, typical of many published by railroad and steamship companies, provided advice for gold seekers bound for the Klondike.

So many people, ladened with tons of supplies, were clamoring to reach the goldfields that there weren't enough boats to carry them all. Vessels that were barely seaworthy were pressed into service. On board the ships, people were crowded together in uncomfortable and unsanitary conditions. Many ships were so overcrowded that passengers had to eat standing up and sleep two and three to a bunk.

In addition to being dangerously overloaded, some ships were piloted by captains unfamiliar with Alaska's treacherous waterways. Surprisingly, there was only one fatal accident. A ship carrying dynamite blew up, killing all sixty-five people aboard.

The crowded ships sailed to one of two ports in Alaska. The easiest and most expensive route to the Klondike was to sail up the Pacific Coast to St. Michael, an Eskimo village near the mouth of the mighty Yukon River. There, passengers boarded smaller boats for the long trip up the Yukon, which meanders nearly two thousand miles across the vast territory of Alaska. The voyage from Seattle took about six weeks and could be made only between late spring and early fall when the Yukon River wasn't frozen.

The most popular route was much cheaper and could be made any time of the year. It was a five-day, one-thousand-mile voyage along the island-dotted coast of British Columbia and southeast Alaska to the new boom town of Skagway. From there, the Klondikers had to climb the rugged Coast Mountains and cross five hundred and fifty miles of wilderness to reach Dawson. The journey was long, hard, and often dangerous.

Most Klondikers "packed," or carried, their supplies over the Coast Mountains. Local Indian men and women, such as the two people in the foreground, were also hired as packers.

The Trail to the Klondike

O N JULY 26, 1897, only ten days after the world had first heard of the big Klondike gold strike, a steamship dropped anchor at the mouth of the Skagway River. This ship was full of desperate gold seekers, the first wave of an army of Klondikers who were about to invade the peaceful land.

Until that July day, this land had been a wilderness. The Territory of Alaska, which the United States had purchased from Russia only thirty years before, was thought of as a bitterly cold and uninhabitable place. But its long southern coast is warmed by ocean currents and lined by lush evergreen and rain forests. Streams full of salmon keep the many bald eagles and grizzly bears well fed.

For countless centuries, this coast had been inhabited by Indians. They first saw white people only in the late eighteenth century when Russians, who were the first Europeans to explore and claim Alaska, hunted sea otters along the coast. When the Klondike Gold Rush began, few white people lived in the area. At Dyea Inlet, nine miles north of Skagway, several white men operated a trading post where they bartered with the Indians trading food and trinkets for beaver, otter, seal, and other valuable furs.

The natural harbors at the mouths of the Skagway and Dyea rivers were only six hundred miles from Dawson. Today the Dyea River is called the Taiya River. From each harbor, a trail led up and over the Coast Mountains. Crossing these mountains, a forbidding wall of seven- to eight-thousand-foot peaks that often are swept by violent storms, was the most difficult part of the long trip to the Klondike.

Nearly every day in August of 1897, steamships from Victoria, Seattle, and San Francisco arrived at Skagway and Dyea. Waves of determined Klondikers bearing tons of supplies charged ashore. By September, Skagway and Dyea were bustling gold-rush towns.

The new town of Skagway only two weeks after the first ship full of Klondikers had landed. Just a few months later this street was lined with wood-frame buildings.

Canvas tents and hastily built wood-frame buildings lined their dirt streets. Before long, each town had permanent populations of several thousand people who sold lodging and food and supplies to the swarms of Klondikers.

Skagway, according to an officer of Canada's Northwest Mounted Police, "was about the roughest place in the world." Without a police force or government, it became a den for crooks skilled at separating newcomers from their money and valuable supplies. Fights and shootings occurred daily. One of Alaska's most infamous criminals, Jefferson "Soapy" Smith, was known as the "dictator" of Skagway. Smith and his gang controlled the town for over a year, until he was killed in a shootout.

For most of the newly arrived gold seekers, neither Skagway nor Dyea, which was only somewhat safer than Skagway, were places to linger. They hurried through these towns and began the strenuous journey over the mountains.

People tried a variety of imaginative ways to transport their supplies across the steep mountains. They used wagons, sleds, dogs, horses, oxen, and goats. But the majority of Klondikers "packed," or carried, their supplies on their backs.

Jack London, the writer, was among the first Klondikers to cross the mountains. In a letter to a friend, the twenty-one-year-old Californian described how he planned to pack his supplies along the thirty-three-mile Dyea Trail to Lake Lindeman:

"I expect to carry 100 lbs. to the load on good trail & on the worst, 75 lbs. That is, for every mile to the lakes, I will have to travel from 20 to 30 miles. I have 1000 lbs. in my outfit. I have to divide it into from 10 to fifteen loads according to the trail. I take a load a mile & come back empty that makes two miles. . . . Am certain we will reach the lake in 30 days."

A narrow section of the first part of the Skagway Trail.

Some Klondikers lightened their loads by hiring Indian men, women, and children as packers. For many years the local Indians had been bargaining with Russian fur traders. They used that negotiating experience well during the gold rush, charging up to a dollar a pound for packing supplies.

At first, the best route across the mountains appeared to be the Skagway Trail through White Pass. It was some forty-five miles long and only twenty-nine hundred feet above sea level at its highest point, White Pass. The trail, following the Skagway River through the mountains, wound through forests and bogs, up steep, boulder-strewn hills, and along the edges of tall cliffs. The Klondikers hiked the trail, and those who could afford the expense hired horses to carry their supplies.

One of the saddest stories of the Klondike Gold Rush was the fate of the pack horses. Thousands of horses were shipped to Alaska to pack supplies up the steep mountains. Some were wild, others were old, and most were ill suited for the work they had to do. Poorly fed and badly overworked, many horses died cruel deaths. They were forced to work for days without rest. Pack horses that dropped from exhaustion were often left on the trail where they died slowly.

Just a few weeks after the rush began, the last stretch of the Skagway Trail was lined with the carcasses and bones of over two thousand horses. The Skagway Trail became known as the "Dead Horse Trail." This new name was a grim reminder of the

So many horses died on the Skagway Trail that people began calling it the "Dead Horse Trail."

This Klondiker's face shows the weariness of the three-month trip across the mountains.

single-minded determination of the Klondikers to reach the gold fields at any cost. It is probably fortunate, for the horses at least, that torrential rains closed the Skagway Trail for most of the fall of 1897.

During the winter of 1897–1898, some twenty-two thousand Klondikers, nearly half of all the people in the gold rush, hiked the thirty-three mile Dyea Trail and crossed the mountains at Chilkoot Pass. The Dyea Trail was an exhausting uphill climb from sea level to thirty-seven hundred feet.

The first five miles of the Dyea Trail followed a path called "Wagon Road" along the gravel bed of the shallow Dyea River. Wagon Road ended at a place called "Finnegan's Point" where there was a blacksmith, restaurant, hotel, and saloon. Along the trail, wherever there was a suitable place to pitch a tent or build a cabin, people had set up crude restaurants, hotels, and stores to profit from the multitudes of Klondikers.

After Finnegan's Point, the trail passed through a canyon that had been carved by the Dyea River. Known simply as the "Canyon," this two-mile stretch of narrow trail was strewn with boulders and driftwood. The first Klondikers who passed through the Canyon were so happy to have it behind them that they named the next stopping place Pleasant Camp.

As the trail climbed higher and higher, the trees became shorter and scarcer between Pleasant Camp and the next resting place, Sheep Camp. Adding to their burden, Klondikers had to carry wood if they wanted to build fires for warmth or cooking near the treeless summit.

Sheep Camp had been a popular campsite for men who hunted the many mountain sheep that lived among the craggy cliffs. During the gold rush, Sheep Camp became a small town with a constantly changing population that numbered as many as fifteen hundred people at any one time. They lived in tents and roughly constructed cabins huddled closely together. Here, several tent stores sold rope, rifles, hay, tobacco, firewood, and just about anything else that a Klondiker might want or need.

Crude hotels and restaurants catered to the crowds of weary men and women who were hiking the trail. One hotel owner, a Wisconsin farmer who had run out of money before reaching the Klondike, served five hundred meals a day and sold sleeping space

The makeshift community of Sheep Camp on Dyea Trail.

Tent stores, like this one, sold food, rope, tools, and other items people might need on the trail. This is a stereograph, a pair of photographs which gives a three-dimensional effect when looked at through a special viewer. Stereographs were popular in the nineteenth century.

on the floor of his small cabin to as many as forty people a night.

For three miles beyond Sheep Camp, the trail became steeper and steeper until it reached the last flat piece of ground before Chilkoot Pass. It was called the "Scales" because the Klondikers weighed their supplies there. This narrow spot, not much bigger than several football fields, was covered by stacks of canvas bags containing thousands of pounds of supplies that had to be carried up the final and steepest part of the Dyea Trail.

In many ways it was easier to cross the steep Coast Mountains in the winter when Klondikers could walk over frozen rivers and use sleds.

Above the Scales loomed a sheer, thousand-foot hill where, in the winter, fifteen hundred steps were cut in the frozen snow. These steps were named, by some unknown Klondiker with a good sense of irony, the "Golden Stairs." Climbing those steep steps with at least fifty pounds of supplies took most people six hours or more. Nearly every day of the long winter of 1897–1898, a solid line of Klondikers stretched from the bottom to the top of the Golden Stairs. Each person had to make the strenuous climb at least a dozen times. Coming down was easy. People just slid down the icy slope on the seat of their pants.

The most famous scenes of the Klondike Gold Rush are of the line of people climbing the "Golden Stairs" to Chilkoot Pass.

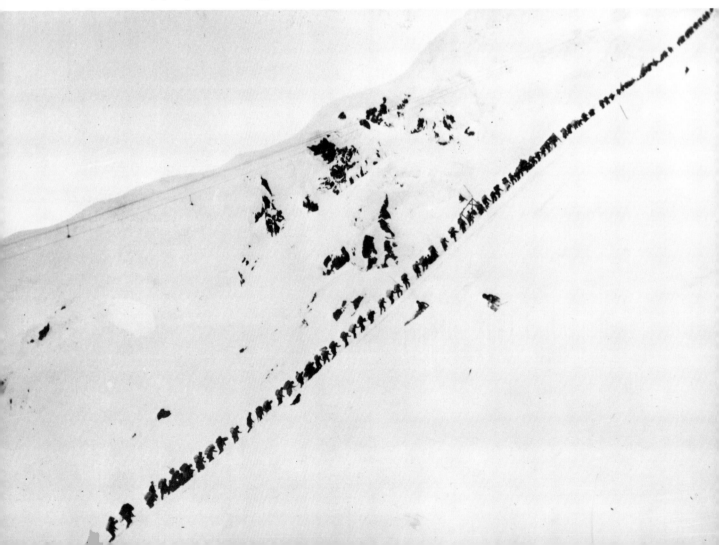

The weather at the summit was often quite severe. Strong winds constantly blew through the pass. During the summer, rain would fall for days. During the winter, snow storms would dump four to five feet of wet snow on the ground in just a few hours. The snow accumulated in drifts as deep as seventy feet, making avalanches a constant danger. In April of 1898, a storm piled six feet of wet snow on the mountain slopes, and an early morning avalanche swept down the mountain and buried a section of the Dyea Trail, killing over sixty men and women.

At the top of the Golden Stairs, was Chilkoot Pass and the border between Canada and the United States. There, every Klondiker and his supplies were checked by the Northwest Mounted Police. Today called the Royal Canadian Mounted Police and popularly known as the "Mounties," the Northwest Mounted Police was formed in the mid-nineteenth century to bring law and order to Canada's vast Northwest Territories.

The Mounties established border checkpoints at both White and Chilkoot passes in early 1898 because mass starvation was threatening the people living along the upper Yukon River. That winter the region's population had nearly doubled. Nobody had planned for so many newcomers. As a result, the trading posts ran out of food before midwinter. More food couldn't be shipped up the frozen Yukon until the river thawed in May. Some people starved to death, and hundreds more barely survived the long winter on meager diets of beans and flour. The shortage was so severe that the Mounties wouldn't even arrest a criminal unless he had enough food to feed himself during his captivity.

At the checkpoint, officers of the Northwest Mounted Police examined all Klondikers to make sure they had enough warm clothing, money, and food to last six or more months. Those who lacked the required supplies were turned back.

Chilkoot Pass in the winter of 1898. The men in uniform and wearing pointed hats are Mounties.

Clearing the Canadian checkpoint must have felt like a major achievement. The Klondikers had spent three months struggling up steep and rocky trails with fifty pounds or more on their backs. They had lived on a monotonous diet of beans and pancakes, slept on the wet and cold ground, and seldom had a chance to wash their clothes or even to bathe. But their sense of achievement must have been tempered by the knowledge that this wretched ordeal did not end at the checkpoint. After Chilkoot Pass, the Klondikers still had another seventeen miles of the Dyea Trail to hike. But this part was all downhill and easier. The trail ended at Lake Bennett.

This lake is connected by One Mile River to Lake Lindeman, where the Skagway Trail ended. These connecting lakes are the

Klondikers building boats beside Lake Bennett.

headwaters of the Yukon River. The two trails both ended at the lakes because the easiest and quickest way to reach Dawson was to build a boat and float down the Yukon. Most of the Klondikers who rushed north and crossed the Coast Mountains that fall did not reach the gold-rush city until late spring of the following year. But by late October of 1897, the lakes and the river were frozen. After the difficult trip across the mountains, thousands of Klondikers had to spend a frigid winter living in canvas tents beside the lakes. They had to wait until breakup, the time when the ice covering the lakes and rivers began to crack and flow downstream.

By spring of 1898, thousands of small white tents dotted the shores of Lake Bennett and Lake Lindeman. The surrounding hills, once quiet, echoed with the constant sounds of sawing and hammering. Everybody was cutting down trees and building boats to carry them and their supplies across the lakes and down the Yukon River five hundred and fifty miles to Dawson.

On May 29, the ice began to crack, and hundreds of newly made boats braved the ice floes in the race to be first to the goldfields. Two days later most of the ice had flowed down river, and several thousand boats, canoes, skiffs, kayaks, and rafts began their two-week voyage down the Yukon. The flotilla carried some fifteen thousand people and thirty million pounds of supplies.

Klondikers on their way down the Yukon River to Dawson.

Fortunately for this ragtag navy of inexperienced sailors, the journey was dangerous at only one point. At Miles Canyon, the water rushed between high rock walls, and the churning current created a powerful whirlpool. One boat was trapped in this whirlpool, spinning around and around for six hours before its passengers managed to free themselves from the water's grip. Others weren't so lucky. At Miles Canyon a hundred and fifty boats wrecked and ten men drowned.

To prevent more deaths, the Northwest Mounted Police set up a checkpoint above Miles Canyon. They inspected every boat before it went through the canyon to make sure it had been properly loaded to reduce the chance of wrecking. Women and children were told to walk around the canyon. No one else drowned and many fewer boats wrecked.

Thousands of people struggled up and over the Coast Mountains and floated down the lakes and rivers. Their long journey ended at the gold-rush city of Dawson, which offered comfort and excitement and, maybe, wealth.

Dawson, early in the summer of 1898, when hundreds of newcomers were arriving daily.

The Gold-Rush City of Dawson

———————◆———————

DAWSON DID not exist before 1896. But by the fall of 1898 it was one of the largest, liveliest, and most cosmopolitan cities in the Northwest. In some ways Dawson resembled other North American cities, but in many other ways it was unique.

Dawson was a city where everything was scarce except money. With that in mind, some of the thousands of people who arrived there during the hectic summer of 1898 hoped to strike it rich without ever mining for gold.

One man arrived in a boat loaded with thousands of pounds of candy, oranges, lemons, bananas, and cucumbers, scarce foods that sold quickly. Another brought his cow and sold milk for thirty dollars a gallon. Someone else arrived with twenty-four hundred eggs and sold them all for thirty-six hundred dollars. One of the most unusual cargoes was a load of irresistible kittens that were sold for fifteen dollars each to lonely miners.

With the arrival of so many newcomers that summer, Dawson grew rapidly from a city of tents to a city of log cabins and wood-frame buildings inhabited by some twenty thousand people. During the day, busy Broadway and Wall Street were like big bazaars where it was possible to buy mining equipment, books, tuxedos, furs, ice cream, and sundry other items.

At night, crowds of men sauntered along Front Street where several blocks of two- and three-story buildings with elaborate fronts housed lively dance halls, saloons, and casinos, with names like Combination, Pioneer, Monte Carlo, and Aurora. Inside, dance-hall girls named Diamond Tooth Gertie and Snake Hips Lulu sold dances for a dollar each. All along Front Street, the lively crowds and the tinkling of pianos created a carnival atmosphere.

Before it was three years old, Dawson had many of the comforts found in older cities, such as telephones, running water, steam heat, and electricity. Swank restaurants served elaborate dinners and expensive European wines. The city had three hospitals, dozens of physicians, and scores of lawyers.

Many people were drawn to Dawson because jobs were plentiful. And all jobs, from lawyer to laundress, paid exceptionally well. While the average wage in the United States was less than two dollars a day, in Dawson gold dust weighers earned twenty dollars a day, teamsters earned one hundred dollars a day, and lawyers earned one hundred and fifty dollars a day.

In addition to its high wages, Dawson was unique in other ways. While the city's two banks readily exchanged Canadian dollars for gold, many people preferred to use gold dust rather than money for their purchases. Restaurants, stores, and other businesses kept scales on their counters to weigh the dust, which was worth sixteen dollars an ounce.

Gold dust was so commonly used that it found its way into nearly everything. Women who washed clothes for a living sometimes scooped twenty dollars or more in gold from the bottom of

A roulette wheel in a casino in Dawson. Prospectors gathered in casinos and dance halls for entertainment.

A dance-hall girl.
Her stage name was
Snake Hips Lulu.

Because prospectors often paid their bills with gold dust, stores kept a small set of scales on the counter to weigh it.

The price of all fruits and vegetables in Dawson was very high because nothing could be grown locally.

Even in faraway Dawson, children had to go to school.

their washtubs at the end of the day. During the Great Depression of the 1930s, jobless people made money by gathering the gold dust from under Dawson's stores and sidewalks where it had fallen between floorboards many years before.

While Dawson produced a lot of gold, just about everything else had to be imported. There were no local farms that grew vegetables or raised chickens and cows for eggs, milk, and meat. No local manufacturers made clothing or shoes. Nearly everything people needed for day-to-day living had to be shipped from cities in southern Canada or in the United States.

The nearest cities were Victoria and Seattle. Overland, they were only two thousand miles away. But there were no overland supply routes, so food and other necessities had to be shipped up the Pacific Coast to St. Michael and then up the Yukon River to Dawson. It was a five-thousand-mile trip that took at least six weeks.

For supplies and transportation, the Yukon River was an important lifeline for the whole Yukon Territory. By the autumn of 1898, there were sixty boats steaming up and down the river. Some, like the *Suzy* and the *Bonanza King*, were grand Mississippi-style riverboats built in Louisville, Kentucky. But these boats sailed only from June to October when the river wasn't frozen. For the rest of the year Dawson was entirely isolated.

Because of this isolation, people sorely missed news about the rest of the world. They were particularly interested in the Spanish-American War, which had begun in February of 1898. News traveled between other cities by telegraph and by telephone. Although Dawson had local telephone service, there were no wires across the vast wilderness to connect it with cities to the south. Newspapers, by the time they reached Dawson, were at least a month old.

But any news was welcome news. One newcomer auctioned a five-week-old Seattle newspaper to the highest bidder. It was sold for fifty dollars to a clever miner who hired a good public speaker to read the newspaper to an audience. He charged one dollar per person for the privilege of hearing last month's news and drew a crowd of over a hundred people.

Dawson, unlike Skagway which fit the image of the wild gold-rush town, was a remarkably law-abiding city. The two hundred Northwest Mounted Police garrisoned in the region maintained strict law and order. No one in Dawson was permitted to carry a revolver without a license, and few people were given licenses. There were only two murders and a few cases of assault. Of the one hundred and thirty-seven deaths recorded in the Yukon Territory by the Mounties in 1898, most were from disease, mainly typhoid fever.

Working on Sundays was strictly against the law. Saloons and dance halls had to close one minute before midnight Saturday and weren't allowed to reopen until two o'clock Monday morning. It was even against the law to fish or to cut firewood on Sunday.

Petty thievery was the most common crime. Dog stealing and using vile language were other common crimes. A person convicted of one of these crimes was either fined, ordered to leave town, or sentenced to chopping firewood to heat government offices.

All in all, Dawson was a remarkably safe and civilized city. According to Samuel B. Steele, the local commander of the Northwest Mounted Police, "Acts of indecency are severely punished and it can safely be said that any man, woman, or child, may walk at any time of the night to any portion of this large camp with perfect safety from insult. . . ."

OPPOSITE: *At the height of the rush, some sixty paddle-wheel steamers cruised the Yukon River.*

These men were among the two hundred Northwest Mounted Police who kept law and order in Dawson and the surrounding region.

Samuel B. Steele, superintendent of the Northwest Mounted Police in Dawson, was so tough that he was nicknamed the "Lion of the Yukon."

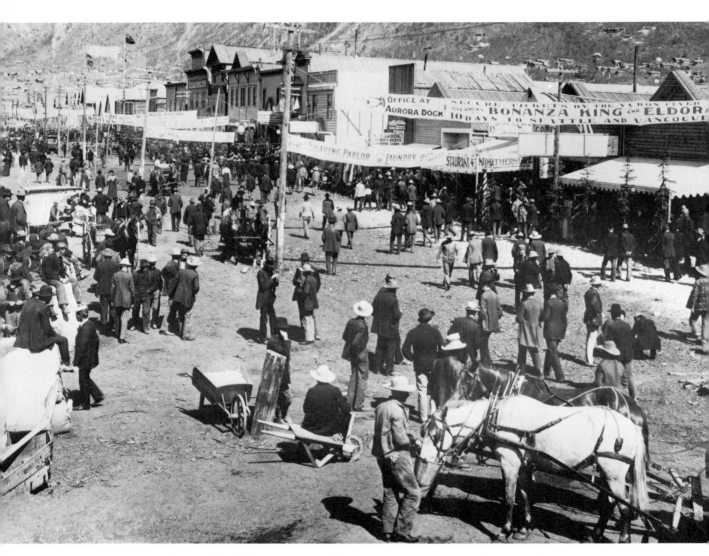

By the end of the summer of 1898 Dawson was a busy and prosperous city.

Like any other city, Dawson had its prominent citizens. Big Alex McDonald was called "King of the Klondike" because he was by far the richest man in Dawson. He had spent many years mining for gold in Colorado and in southeast Alaska before moving to the Upper Yukon in 1895. McDonald didn't like the idea of actually digging for gold. Instead, he made a fortune during the gold rush buying claims and letting other men work them in return for a share of the gold. As he grew wealthy from his choice claims, Big Alex bought steamboats and businesses. By 1898, the King of the Klondike was worth an estimated five million dollars.

Another famous Dawson resident was Belinda Mulroney. Giving up a job as a ship's stewardess, the intrepid woman crossed the Coast Mountains and floated by boat to the new gold-rush town in the spring of 1897. She brought with her five thousand dollars worth of cotton clothing and hot-water bottles, which she sold in Dawson for thirty thousand dollars. Mulroney wisely invested her profits in a lunch counter, in building cabins to sell to newcomers, and in a roadhouse, a kind of restaurant and bar, in the goldfields outside of Dawson.

By the summer of 1898, Mulroney had enough money to build the Fairview, the city's fanciest hotel. It had electric lights, steam heat, and a Turkish bath. At dinner, dining room tables were set with silver, china, and crystal. In the background, a chamber orchestra played Bach and Mozart.

The luxurious Fairview and other city comforts made it easy to forget that Dawson existed only because of the gold being dug from the surrounding streams and hills. Life was quite different for the several thousand people who lived and labored in the mining camps.

A miner entertains himself with a well-worn deck of cards.

Digging for Gold

IN THE SUMMER of 1898, newcomers flooded the already crowded streams and valleys of the Klondike. By July the busy claims office in Dawson had registered over nine thousand claims. For eighty miles, these claims lined Bonanza and Klondike creeks, where over five thousand people worked hard and lived simply.

These miners lived in tents until they had time to build small cabins. The typical log cabin measured twelve by sixteen feet and had a window at each end. It was sparsely furnished with home-made chairs, a table, and a bed; heated by a woodburning stove; and lit by a kerosene lamp.

Life in the goldfields, unlike life in Dawson, was a monotonous routine with little entertainment. At roadhouses, like Belinda Mulroney's, miners could gamble and buy meals and drinks. But by February, when the temperature dropped to a bone-chilling fifty below zero and it was depressingly dark twenty-four hours a day, the roadhouses would run low on supplies. Their last shipment had arrived in October, and the next shipment wouldn't arrive until June.

Tents, cabins, and sluices lined Bonanza Creek for many miles.

The most reliable, and cheapest, kind of entertainment was talking. Prospectors exchanged rumors and stories about the latest gold strike or about the huge nugget someone had found. Like people everywhere, they talked about the weather, which was so cold one month that no one could go outside for three days. And because the miners lived on a steady diet of beans, flour, and an occasional tin of canned meat, everybody talked lovingly about food. They dreamed aloud of strolling into Dawson with a sack full of gold and ordering champagne and oysters for breakfast.

The monotony and harshness of life in the goldfields was made worse by the bleak landscape. Before the gold rush, the rolling hills along the Klondike River had been covered by birch and spruce trees. But by late 1898, most of the trees for miles around had been cut for firewood and for building cabins. Gray smoke from thousands of fires often filled the valley like a heavy fog, and mounds of gravel and dirt lined the streams and creeks.

At first, all of the mining in the Klondike was of a type known as "placer" or "streambed" prospecting. That meant that gold was mined either in streams, or because streams often changed course, nearby beneath old streambeds.

Digging for gold was not the only way to make money in the goldfields.

In the goldfields, a miner's work was never done.

These streams, untold centuries earlier, had flowed over a large deposit of gold called a "lode." The water broke pieces of the soft metal from the lode and washed them downstream. The flowing water and constant bumping against rocks broke the gold into small nuggets and fine grains, called "dust," that were scattered along the bottoms of streams.

Locating and unearthing this gold was not easy. The Klondikers randomly dug deep holes in or near a streambed. They called this "drifting," and it was usually done in the winter. Because the earth was frozen hard, miners had to burn fires all night to thaw the ground that was to be dug during the day.

The prospectors dug deeper and deeper into the hard ground until they hit bedrock, which was any type of rock dense enough to hold gold. On one claim, bedrock might be only twelve feet below the surface. On another claim, it might be fifty feet below the surface. Digging just one hole in the frozen ground could take as long as thirty days. Several dozen holes often had to be dug before gold was found or before the claim was abandoned.

As the prospectors dug, they frequently checked samples of their gravel for gold. They were looking for "pay dirt," earth that yielded enough gold to make digging there profitable. In the Klondike, an average of ten cents worth of gold in each sample was considered pay dirt.

The sifting of pay dirt required lots of water, so it was only done in the summer when water wasn't frozen. By late May, the temperature along the Klondike was warm enough so that the mounds of dirt that had accumulated over the long winter could be sifted for gold.

Mining gold was hard, dirty work.

These miners are panning pay dirt in the comfort of their cabin.

The prospectors separated the gold from dirt and gravel by rocker, sluice, or gold pan. All three methods were very crude, and the miners overlooked as much gold as they found.

A rocker, which resembled a cradle, was a wooden box on curved legs. The bottom of the box was punched with holes and beneath that was a shelf called an "apron." Prospectors partially filled the rocker with pay dirt, then rocked it back and forth while water was poured in. The rocking and the water caused the heavy gold, along with some of the rock and dirt, to fall through the holes onto the apron. Then the prospectors very carefully picked over the dirt in the apron looking for gold nuggets and bits of gold dust.

To separate the fine particles of gold dust from the dirt, both were put into a bucket of water with quicksilver (another name for mercury), which attracts gold like a magnet attracts iron. Then, stuck together, the gold and quicksilver were taken out of the water and heated. The quicksilver quickly dissolved, leaving a mass of gold.

A sluice was better than a rocker for sifting through large quantities of dirt. A sluice was several, long interconnecting wooden boxes about a foot wide with high sides. The bottom of each box was a removable section of wooden ribs, called "riffles,"

This man is looking carefully for flakes of gold caught on the riffles of the sluice.

which resembled an old-fashioned washboard. Pay dirt was shoveled into the sluice, and water ran through the box flushing dirt and gravel downward. The riffles caught the heavy gold and some gravel, which then had to be carefully picked over by hand.

Sluice boxes needed steep, downhill streams of water. When a stream wasn't naturally steep enough, a dam was built to raise the water level, and the water was often shared by several claims.

Gold pans were an important part of every prospector's equipment. They were used to check small quantities of dirt. The process is called "panning." The pan was partially filled with gravel and dirt. Water was added, and the mixture was swished around and around to wash the dirt from the gravel and from whatever gold might be there. Meanwhile, the prospector would peer into the pan hoping to spot a flake or a nugget.

Gold pans were especially useful in placer or streambed prospecting. At first, prospectors believed all of the Klondike's gold would be found in or beside streams. But some smart miners discovered differently.

Several prospectors decided to dig in the hills several hundred feet above Bonanza Creek. Streams can drastically change course, these men reasoned, so Bonanza Creek at one time might have been much higher.

The sourdoughs, who considered themselves wise in the ways of gold, scoffed that only the greenest *cheechako* (CHEE-cha-ko), an Indian word meaning "greenhorn," would look for gold on top of a hill. It turned out that the hills, which were named French, Gold, and Cheechako, were rich with gold.

The Klondike prospectors unearthed millions of dollars worth of gold nuggets and gold dust. In only five months, between July and November of 1898, the United States mints in Seattle and

San Francisco received ten million dollars worth of Klondike gold. In 1899, the mints received sixteen million dollars in gold. The peak year was 1900, when the mints received twenty-two million dollars in gold.

Over the next fifty years, the region produced five hundred million dollars worth of gold. But for the men and women who struggled north in 1897 and 1898, the Klondike Gold Rush ended much sooner.

Klondike gold after it had been melted and shaped into bricks.

Construction of the railroad from Skagway across the rugged mountains to Whitehorse helped big companies take over gold mining in the Klondike.

The Gold Rush Ends

$\mathbf{A}$LTHOUGH MILLIONS of dollars worth of gold was still buried in the hills around Dawson, by mid-1899 the frenzied gold rush had ended. The Klondike Gold Rush had lasted only three years, but its legacy endures to this day.

Gold mining remained a major industry in the Klondike region for over fifty years. But after 1899, most of the gold was mined by big companies with their headquarters in distant cities like Montreal, Chicago, and New York. These companies took over mining in the Klondike after a railroad was blasted out of the rugged mountains from Skagway through White Pass to the new town of Whitehorse. Built in the remarkably short time of fourteen months, the railroad enabled mining companies to move large gold dredges across the Coast Mountains. These efficient machines were operated by only a few men, but they could do the work of hundreds of men by sifting through tons of gravel a day.

After the mining companies took over, little gold was mined by sourdoughs wielding picks, shovels, and gold pans. But many

After 1899, gold dredges like this one did most of the mining on the Klondike creeks.

prospectors clung to the dream of unearthing a fortune, or they simply enjoyed the gold-mining life. These sourdoughs joined other, smaller rushes in both Canada and Alaska. In the summer of 1898, gold was discovered two thousand miles across Alaska on the beach at Cape Nome. The following summer, some eight thousand Klondikers in Dawson clamored aboard paddle-wheel steamers bound for the new tent city of Nome. Three years later, other Klondikers joined the gold rush to the Chena River, an area near the middle of Alaska which would become the city of Fairbanks.

The decline of Dawson began in the summer of 1899 when eight thousand people boarded paddle-wheel steamers to rush to the new gold strike at Cape Nome.

*Belinda Mulroney,
some years after she
had left Dawson.*

One of the people who participated in that 1902 Fairbanks rush was Belinda Mulroney, the Dawson hotel owner. She had used her considerable business skills to become the successful manager of the Klondike's largest gold-mining company. But she quit that job for the excitement of the Fairbanks gold rush. Eight years later, Mulroney retired to a quieter life on a ranch near Yakima, Washington.

Another veteran of the Klondike who retired was George Carmack. After separating from his Indian wife, Carmack and a new wife moved to the growing port city of Vancouver, British Columbia, where they invested their money in real estate.

For some prospectors, the lure of gold remained irresistible. With little luck, Robert Henderson continued digging in the creeks and streams of the Klondike until he died in 1933. Henderson's son lived his life in Dawson searching in vain for the gold that had always eluded his father.

Big Alex McDonald kept investing in mining claims, but never equaled his earlier success. By the time he died, the King of the Klondike had lost most of his fortune.

Charlie and Jim, George Carmack's Indian companions, stayed close to their ancestral home, but gave up many of their native customs. Charlie purchased a hotel and operated it until he died an alcoholic. And Jim, although he had made a fortune from his claims, became obsessed by gold. He spent the rest of his life unsuccessfully prospecting for another gold strike like the one at Bonanza Creek.

After most prospectors had moved on or given up, Robert Henderson continued his quest for gold in the Yukon Territory.

Charlie, soon after he became wealthy from his claim on Bonanza Creek.

Jim, the well-dressed man holding the gold pan, with his wife, daughter, and friends in a 1901 photograph.

George Washington Carmack, sitting third from the left, at a birthday party in Dawson.

Alex McDonald, Belinda Mulroney, and the other men and women who ventured into the northern wilderness to prospect for gold were important pioneers of Alaska and northwest Canada. These restless people were part of the mass migration across North America after the Civil War. One of the main reasons for this mass movement was the search for gold. Eagerly seeking this precious metal, North Americans by the tens of thousands rushed west to the Pacific Ocean and then north nearly to the Arctic Circle.

These pioneers followed a pattern that characterized the many gold rushes in the last half of the nineteenth century. During those fifty years, thousands of people rushed to gold strikes in British Columbia, California, Colorado, Nevada, and other parts of western North America. Along the way they created towns, cities, and states.

Similarly, the population of Dawson and the surrounding area had multiplied from a few hundred prospectors at the beginning of 1896 to fifty thousand Klondikers at the height of the gold rush in 1898. That year, recognizing the need for local government, the Canadian Parliament in Ottawa carved the Yukon Territory out of the vast Northwest Territories. The territorial capital remained in Dawson until the 1950s, when it moved south to the more populated town of Whitehorse.

Of the major towns and cities in Alaska and the Yukon Territory, only one was not created by a gold rush. Anchorage, Alaska's largest city, began as a construction camp for the Alaska Railroad. But Juneau, Dawson, Whitehorse, Nome, and Fairbanks all began as gold-rush towns.

In the early twentieth century, there were several more gold rushes in North America. But the continent has never witnessed another one as big or as dramatic as the great Klondike Gold Rush.

Leaving the Klondike, these prospectors are headed for a new gold strike near Whitehorse.

Bibliography

Acknowledgments and Photo Credits

Index

Bibliography

Becker, Ethel A. *Klondike '98: E. A. Hegg's Gold Rush Album*. Portland, Ore.: Metropolitan, 1967.

Berton, Pierre. *Klondike: The Last Great Gold Rush 1896–1899*. Toronto: McClelland and Stewart, 1958. Revised Edition. Toronto: McClelland and Stewart, 1987.

Hinton, A., and Philip H. Godsell. *The Yukon*. Philadelphia: Macrae Smith, 1955.

Howard, S. W. *The Pictorial History of the Royal Canadian Police*. New York: McGraw-Hill, 1973.

Hulley, Clarence C. *Alaska 1741–1953*. Portland, Ore.: Binforts and Mort, 1953.

Kirk, Robert C. *Twelve Months in the Klondike*. London: W. Heinemann, 1899.

Lynch, Jeremiah. *Three Years in the Klondike*. London: E. Arnold, 1904.

Macdonald, Alexander. *In Search of Eldorado*. Philadelphia: G. W. Jacobs & Co., 1907.

May, Robin. *The Gold Rushes: From California to the Klondike.* Melbourne (Australia): Macmillan, 1977.

Ogilvie, William. *Early Days on the Yukon and the Story of Its Gold Finds.* Ottawa: Thorburn and Abbot, 1913.

Rea, Kenneth J. *The Political Economy of the Canadian North.* Toronto: University of Toronto Press, 1968.

Steele, Colonel S. B. *Forty Years in Canada.* London: H. Jenkins Ltd., 1915.

Story, Norah. *Oxford Companion to Canadian History and Literature.* Toronto and New York: Oxford University Press, 1967.

Vicker, Ray. *The Realms of Gold.* New York: Scribner's, 1975.

Wells, E. Hazard. *Magnificence and Misery: A First Hand Account of the 1897 Klondike Gold Rush.* Edited by Randall M. Dodd. Garden City, N.Y.: Doubleday, 1984.

Suggested Readings

Becker, Ethel A. *Klondike '98: E. A. Hegg's Gold Rush Album.* Portland, Ore.: Metropolitan, 1967.

Berton, Pierre. *Klondike: The Last Great Gold Rush 1896–1899.* Toronto: McClelland and Stewart, 1958. Revised Edition. Toronto: McClelland and Stewart, 1987.

London, Jack. *Call of the Wild.* New York: Penquin, 1983.

Wells, E. Hazard. *Magnificence and Misery: A First Hand Account of the 1897 Klondike Gold Rush.* Edited by Randall M. Dodd. Garden City, N.Y.: Doubleday, 1984.

Acknowledgments and Photo Credits

Archivists and librarians are among the most patient and helpful people in creation. My thanks to Richard H. Engeman, University of Washington Libraries; Elaine Miller, the Washington State Historical Society; Frances A. Hare, Yakima Valley Museum and Historical Society; Judith Breshears, Yukon Libraries and Archives; E. M. Clark, Royal Canadian National Mounted Police; Gloria MacKenzie, Documentary Art and Photography Division, Public Archives Canada.

I've been helped by many staff people whose names I'll never know, so my collective thanks to the staffs of: Pictorial Collections, Bancroft Library, University of California, Berkeley; Museum of History and Industry, Seattle; Prints and Photographs Division, Library of Congress.

The Bancroft Library: page 23.

Library of Congress: pages 20, 26, 27, 32, 63.

Museum of History and Industry, Seattle, Washington: pages 8, 15.

National Archives of Canada: endpapers (negative number C-4489), frontis (negative number C-16460), page 3 (negative number PA-16875), page

11 (negative number PA-28867), page 18 (negative number C-28645), page 28 (negative number C-4489), page 30 (negative number C-1277), page 31 (negative number C-28676), page 38, top photo (negative number C-14477), bottom photo (negative number C-5393), page 44 (negative number C-22074), page 45 (negative number PA-28146), page 46 (negative number C-6648), page 52 (negative number C-68898), page 53 (negative number PA-16276), page 54 (negative number C-5392), page 57 (negative number C-1283), page 58 (negative number C-4331), page 60 (negative number C-20060), page 68 (negative number PA-155254).

Picture Collection, New York Public Library: pages 12, 16.

Royal Canadian Mounted Police: page 61.

Seattle Post-Intelligencer: page 10.

Special Collections Division, University of Washington Libraries: page 4 (negative number 8978). Photo by Winter & Pond, page 7 (negative number 264). Photos by Goetzman, page 34 (negative number 620), page 37 (negative number 3019), page 40 (negative number 3002). Page 39 (Yukon Cities #9, negative number VW 9241). Photo by Nowell, page 42 (negative number 2476A). Photo by Hegg, page 51 (negative number B461).

Washington State Historical Society: introduction photo, pages 22, 24, 48, 50, 55.

Yakima Valley Museum and Historical Association: page 62.

Yukon Libraries and Archives: pages 64, 65, 66.

Index

Note: *Italicized* page numbers indicate illustrations.